Fight Night

Gavin Kostick

methuen | drama

LONDON • NEW YORK • OXFORD • NEW DELHI • SYDNEY

METHUEN DRAMA

Bloomsbury Publishing Plc, 50 Bedford Square, London, WC1B 3DP, UK
Bloomsbury Publishing Inc, 1385 Broadway, New York, NY 10018, USA
Bloomsbury Publishing Ireland, 29 Earlsfort Terrace, Dublin 2,
D02 AY28, Ireland

BLOOMSBURY, METHUEN DRAMA and the Methuen
Drama logo are trademarks of Bloomsbury Publishing Plc.

First published in Great Britain 2025

Bloomsbury Publishing Plc does not have any control over, or responsibility
for, any third-party websites referred to or in this book. All internet addresses
given in this book were correct at the time of going to press. The author and
publisher regret any inconvenience caused if addresses have changed or sites
have ceased to exist, but can accept no responsibility for any such changes.

No rights in incidental music or songs contained in the work are hereby
granted and performance rights for any performance/presentation
whatsoever must be obtained from the respective copyright owners.

All rights whatsoever in this play are strictly reserved and application
for performance etc. should be made before rehearsals begin to Fishamble:
The New Play Company, 3 Great Denmark Street, Dublin 1, Ireland,
D01 NV63 (info@fishamble.com). No performance may
be given unless a licence has been obtained.

A catalogue record for this book is available from the British Library.

Library of Congress Control Number: 2025932889

ISBN: PB: 978-1-3505-5653-9
ePDF: 978-1-3505-5655-3
eBook: 978-1-3505-5654-6

Series: Modern Plays

Typeset by Mark Heslington Ltd, Scarborough, North Yorkshire

For product safety related questions contact
productsafety@bloomsbury.com.

To find out more about our authors and books visit
www.bloomsbury.com and sign up for our newsletters.

ABOUT FISHAMBLE

Fishamble is an Irish theatre company that discovers, develops and produces new plays of national importance with a global reach. It has toured its productions to audiences throughout Ireland, and to twenty-one other countries. It champions the role of the playwright, typically supporting over 50% of the writers of all new plays produced on the island of Ireland each year. Fishamble has received many awards in Ireland and internationally, including an Olivier Award.

'excellent Fishamble . . . Ireland's terrific Fishamble' **Guardian**

'Ireland's leading new writing company' **The Stage**

'the much-loved Fishamble [is] a global brand with international theatrical presence . . . an unswerving force for new writing' **Irish Times**

'the respected Dublin company . . . forward-thinking Fishamble' **New York Times**

'when Fishamble is [in New York], you've got to go' **Time Out New York**

'that great Irish new writing company, Fishamble' **Lyn Gardner, Stage Door**

'the superb Irish company Fishamble' **Scotsman**

'Fishamble puts electricity into the National grid of dreams' **Sebastian Barry**

Fishamble staff: Jim Culleton (Artistic Director and CEO), Eva Scanlan (Executive Director), Gavin Kostick (Literary Manager), Sarah Bragg-Bolger (General Manager), Laura

MacNaughton (Producer), Evie McGuinness (Assistant Producer), Allie Whelan (Marketing, Outreach, and Engagement Manager)

Fishamble board: Peter Finnegan, John McGrane, Louise Molloy, Ronan Nulty, John O'Donnell, Siobhan O'Leary (Chair), Colleen Savage, John Tierney, Denise Walshe

Fishamble is funded by the Arts Council, Dublin City Council, and Culture Ireland.

Fishamble's most recent productions include:

- *Breaking* by Amy Kidd (2024) in Dublin Theatre Festival and on tour

- *Transatlantic Commissions Residency* by Felispeaks, Kwaku Fortune, Jade Jordan and CN Smith (2024) in Dublin and New York, in partnership with the Irish Rep

- *Certain Individual Women* by Julie Morrissy (2024) on national tour

- *Taigh Tŷ Teach* by Eva O'Connor, Màiri Morrison and Mared Llywelyn Williams (2024) in Kerry and touring to Scotland and Wales, in partnership with Theatre Gu Leòr and Theatr Bara Caws

- *In Two Minds* by Joanne Ryan (since 2023) touring in Ireland and UK

- *King* by Pat Kinevane (since 2023) touring in Ireland, UK, Europe and US

- *Heaven* by Eugene O'Brien (since 2022) touring in Ireland, UK and US

- *Outrage* by Deirdre Kinahan (2022 and 2024) touring and online, as part of the Decade of Centenaries

- *The Pride of Parnell Street* by Sebastian Barry (2007–11 and 2022) touring in Ireland and internationally, BBC Audio

- *The Treaty* by Colin Murphy (2021–22) in Ireland, Irish Embassy in London and online as part of the Decade of Centenaries and Seóda Festival

- *Duck Duck Goose* by Caitríona Daly (2021–22) touring in Ireland and online

- *On Blueberry Hill* by Sebastian Barry (2017–21) touring in Ireland, Europe, Off-Broadway, West End, Audible and online

- *Mustard* by Eva O'Connor (since 2020) on tour in Ireland, internationally and online

- *On the Horizon* in association with Dirty Protest, by Shannon Yee, Hefin Robinson, Michael Patrick, Oisín Kearney, Samantha O'Rourke, Ciara Elizabeth Smyth, Connor Allen (2021) online

- *Tiny Plays for a Brighter Future* by Niall Murphy, Signe Lury, Eva-Jane Gaffney (2021) online

- *Embargo* by Deirdre Kinahan (2020) online during Dublin Theatre Festival

- *Tiny Plays 24/7* by Lora Hartin, Maria Popovic, Ciara Elizabeth Smyth, Caitríona Daly, Conor Hanratty, Julia Marks, Patrick O'Laoghaire, Eric O'Brien, Grace Lobo, Ryan Murphy (2020) online

- *The Alternative* by Oisín Kearney and Michael Patrick (2019) on tour to Pavilion Theatre, Draíocht, Belltable, Everyman Theatre, Town Hall Theatre and Lyric Theatre

- *Haughey|Gregory* by Colin Murphy (2018–19) in the Abbey Theatre, Mountjoy Prison, Dáil Éireann, Croke Park and Larkin Community College, as well as on national tour

- *The Humours of Bandon* by Margaret McAuliffe (since 2017) touring in Ireland, UK, US and Australia

- *Rathmines Road* by Deirdre Kinahan (2018) in coproduction with the Abbey Theatre

- *Drip Feed* by Karen Cogan (2018) in coproduction with Soho Theatre, touring in Ireland and UK

- *GPO 1818* by Colin Murphy (2018) to mark the bicentenary of the GPO

- *Maz & Bricks* by Eva O'Connor (2017–18) on national and international tour

- *Forgotten, Silent, Underneath* and *Before* by Pat Kinevane (since 2007, 2011, 2014 and 2018, respectively) touring in Ireland, UK, Europe, US, Australia, New Zealand and online, in English and bilingually in many countries

- *Charolais* by Noni Stapleton (2017) in New York

- *Inside the GPO* by Colin Murphy (2016) performed in the GPO during Easter and screened internationally online

- *Tiny Plays for Ireland and America* by twenty-six writers (2016) at the Kennedy Center, Washington, DC and Irish Arts Center, New York, as part of *Ireland 100*

- *Mainstream* by Rosaleen McDonagh (2016) in coproduction with Project Arts Centre

- *Invitation to a Journey* by David Bolger, Deirdre Gribbin, and Gavin Kostick (2016) in coproduction with CoisCeim, Crash Ensemble and Galway International Arts Festival

- *Little Thing, Big Thing* by Donal O'Kelly (2014–16) touring in Ireland, UK, Europe, US and Australia

- *Swing* by Steve Blount, Peter Daly, Gavin Kostick and Janet Moran (2014–16) touring in Ireland, UK, Europe, US, Australia and New Zealand

- *Bailed Out* by Colin Murphy (2015) on national tour

- *Spinning* by Deirdre Kinahan (2014) at Dublin Theatre Festival

- *The Wheelchair on My Face* by Sonya Kelly (2013–14) touring in Ireland, UK, Europe, and US

Fishamble wishes to thank the following Friends of Fishamble and Corporate Members for their invaluable support:

Alan Ashe, ATM Accounting Services, Dearbhail and Michael Bermingham, Doireann Ní Bhriain, Colette and Barry Breen, John Butler, Betsy Carroll, Breda Cashe, Maura Connolly, Jackie Cronin, Finola Earley, John and Yvonne Healy, Nancy E. Jones, Geoffrey and Jane Keating, Stephen and Susan Lambert, Damian Lane, Angus Laverty, Patrick Lonergan, Sheelagh Malin, Monica McInerney, Patrick McIntyre, Ger McNaughton, Anne McQuillan, Mary Monks Hatch, Liz Morrin, Pat Moylan, Ronan Nulty, Lisney, PwC, Tom O'Connor, Siobhan O'Leary, Andrew and Delyth Parkes, Judy Regan, Royal County Furniture, Jennifer Russell, Eileen Ryan, Colleen Savage, Catherine Santoro, Brian Singleton, William Smith, Eddie Soye and Mary Stephenson.

fishamble.com facebook.com/fishamble twitter.com/fishamble

Acknowledgements

Thanks to the following for their help with this production: Maureen Kennelly, Bea Kelleher, David Parnell, Liz Meaney, Maeve Giles, Ciara Coyne, and all at the Arts Council; Ray Yeates, Sinéad Connolly, and all at Dublin City Council Arts Office; Sharon Barry, Ciaran Walsh, Alison Geraghty, and all at Culture Ireland; all at 3 Great Denmark Street; Elysabeth Kleinhans, Val Day, Brian Beirne, and all at 59E59 Theaters; Mick Mellamphy and all at 1st Irish Festival; Lelia Ruckenstein and James O'Malley; all at Irish Theatre Institute and Dublin Fringe Festival; all those who have helped since this publication went to print.

ABOUT RISE PRODUCTIONS

Rise Productions is a multi-award-winning contemporary theatre company based in Dublin, Ireland, with a focus on new writing and a passionate commitment to national and international touring. Notable productions include Gavin Kostick's 'Dynasty and Destiny' trilogy: *Fight Night* (Best Actor, and Bewley's Little Gem awards, Dublin Fringe, nominated Best New Play, Irish Times Theatre Awards), *The Games People Play* (winner Best New Play, Irish Times Theatre Awards) and *At The Ford*; the critically acclaimed revival of Christian O'Reilly's *The Good Father*; Liz FitzGibbon's *Kicking All The Boxes* and *Weekend Warrior* by Tony Doyle. Digital audio content includes the groundbreaking *Rise Productions: Irish Theatre Podcast*, fantasy adventure *Cobra's Quest* for young audiences, and two ten-part series of *Rise: Audio Drama*.

Fishamble: The New Play Company presents Rise Productions'

FIGHT NIGHT

by Gavin Kostick
co-conceived by Gavin Kostick and Aonghus Óg McAnally

Cast
Aonghus Óg McAnally

Creative Team
Director Bryan Burroughs
Lighting Designer Archer Bradshaw
Based on an original design by Colm Maher
Artistic Director (Fishamble) Jim Culleton
Artistic Director (Rise) Aonghus Óg McAnally

Production Team
Producer Laura MacNaughton
Production Manager Eoin Kilkenny
Marketing Allie Whelan
PR O'Doherty Communications
Cover Artwork Ste Murray
Executive Director (Fishamble) Eva Scanlan

Rehearsals were observed by Ad Astra students from UCD, where Fishamble is theatre company-in-association.

The production runs for approximately 60 minutes, with no interval.

Fight Night was first produced by Rise Productions in Bewley's Café Theatre in 2010. It was written and developed as part of Show in a Bag, an artist development initiative of Dublin Fringe Festival, Fishamble: The New Play Company, and Irish Theatre Institute, to resource theatre makers and actors. It was subsequently toured by Rise Productions in Ireland, Scotland and Finland, and a radio version was recorded for RTÉ 1. Fishamble transferred this production to 59E59 Theaters in New York, as part of 1st Irish Festival, in 2025, to mark the play's fifteenth anniversary.

Gavin Kostick is a playwright, literary manager and independent dramaturg.

His works have been produced nationally and internationally. Favourite works for Fishamble include *The Ash Fire*, *The Flesh Addict*, *The End of The Road* and *Invitation to a Journey* (with CoisCeim and Crash Ensemble). Gavin's next planned work with Fishamble is *The Leap*, a play for young people.

Further works include *This is What We Sang* for Kabosh, *Fight Night*, *The Games People Play* and *At the Ford* for Rise Productions and *Gym Swim Party* with Danielle Galligan in co-production with the O'Reilly Theatre. He wrote the libretto for the opera *The Alma Fetish* composed by Raymond Deane, performed at the National Concert Hall. As a performer he performed *Joseph Conrad's Heart of Darkness: Complete*, a six hour show for Absolut Fringe, Dublin Theatre Festival and the London Festival of Literature at the Southbank.

Gavin is currently the literary manager of Fishamble: The New Play Company, a tutor in playwriting and dramaturgy in both The Lir Academy and Trinity College Dublin as well as being a core mentor on the Tenderfoot Transition Year programme for young writers at the Civic Theatre.

Particular favourite projects that Gavin has initiated and delivered with Fishamble include Show in a Bag (with Dublin Fringe and The Irish Theatre Institute), The New Play Clinic, The Dublin Fringe New Writing Award, Tiny Plays for Ireland and A Play for Ireland.

Both for Fishamble, and as an independent dramaturg, Gavin's projects and works he has supported have gained significant national and international award recognition including amongst others Irish Times Irish Theatre Awards, BBC Stewart Parker Trust, Zebbie Awards, Dublin Fringe Awards, Business to Arts, Olivier, Scotsman Fringe First, Herald Angel and Archangel and New York Critics' Pick.

His own plays have also received similar national and international award recognition.

Gavin has recently completed a new version of *The Odyssey*, supported by Kilkenny Arts Festival, ClassicsNow.

Bryan Burroughs is primarily known for his acting work delivering noteworthy performances in *My Foot/My Tutor* with Articulate Anatomy (Best Male Performance at Dublin Fringe Festival 2004); Barabbas Theatre Company's *Johnny Patterson: The Singing Irish Clown* (Irish Times Theatre Award Best Supporting Actor 2009) and his solo show *Beowulf: The Blockbuster* which originated as a Show in a Bag before Pat Moylan became producer where it toured Ireland, Scotland, Wales, France, Australia, New York and became the number one success of the Edinburgh Fringe 2014 winning the STAGE Award for Acting Excellence.

Other notable productions include *The President* at The Gate Theatre with Hugo Weaving and Olwen Fouéré; *Act Without Words 2* by Samuel Beckett for Company SJ which performed at the Barbican in London and the Centre Culturel Irlandais in Paris. James Joyce's *Ulysses* by Dermot Bolger in 2017/2018 and *The Long Christmas Dinner* by Thornton Wilder at The Abbey Theatre in Dec 2021 and 2022 (nominated for Irish Times Theatre Award Best Ensemble for both productions). He played multiple roles in Conall Morrison's adaptation of Patrick Kavanagh's *Tarry Flynn* for Livin' Dred Theatre Company directed by Aaron Monaghan in 2022, *The Boy Who Talked to Dogs* by Amy Conroy as a Slingsby/Draiocht co-production which played at the 2021 Adelaide Festival and toured Australia for 2022 before its Irish arrival at Dublin Theatre Festival 2023 and subsequent Irish tour followed by his and Aaron Monaghan's adaptation of Charles Dickens' *A Christmas Carol* for Livin' Dred Theatre Company in December 2024.

He played Dad in Jody O Neil's *Grace* with Graffiti Theatre for Cork Midsummer Festival, Dublin Theatre Festival 2024 and Baboro Arts Festival For Children in Autumn 2024. *Grace* was also invited to present an excerpt at Meet the Irish event in the Irish Arts Center in New York in January 2025. He has also been cast in Series Two of Tim Burton's *Wednesday* for Netflix in 2025.

As well as directing *Fight Night* which won Best Actor and the Bewley's Little Gem Award at Dublin Fringe 2010, Bryan has also directed the award winning *The Games People Play* for Rise productions, also written by Gavin Kostick, which won Best New Play at the Irish Times Theatre Awards 2013 and *At the Ford* by Gavin Kostick for Rise at Dublin Theatre Festival 2015.

In January 2025 he directed *The Gas Menagerie* by Caitríona Daly for the 24Hr Play Company at The Abbey Theatre and in March 2025 he directed *The Whispering Chair* by Tara Maria Lovett, a co-production by The Mill Theatre Dundrum and Livin' Dred Theatre Company.

As movement director recent productions include *Considering Matthew Shepard* at the National Concert Hall; Fishamble's *Duck, Duck, Goose*; Druid's *Beauty Queen of Leenane*; Umbrella's *Glowworm*; Fishamble's *Inside the GPO*; Yew Tree's *Alone It Stands*; Pat Moylan's *Stones in his Pockets*; *Tarry Flynn* and *The Skriker* at The Lir Academy; BrokenCrow's *Levin & Levin*; The Abbey Theatre's *Fool For Love* and *The Wake* and Second Age's *Hamlet* and *Macbeth*.

For RTÉ Bryan has appeared on RTÉ Jr's *The Beo Show* teaching drama to young children, written four short stories for the *Tell Me a Story* series, written and performed a Christmas short story for the *Cór Na Nóg* Christmas concert and directed *Fight Night* for RTÉ's Radio Drama season.

Bryan teaches physical theatre at The Lir Academy of Dramatic Art in association with RADA and has taught at NYU Tisch School of the Arts Summer Abroad Programme, The Gaiety School of Acting and The Accademia D'ell Arte in Arezzo, Tuscany.

Aonghus Óg McAnally

Aonghus is a graduate of the Samuel Beckett Centre, Trinity College Dublin and also trained with Anne Bogart's SITI Company in New York. Work while at the Beckett Centre included *Mad Forest, The Dandy Dolls, Interludes* and *Ubu Roi*.

Work at the Abbey Theatre includes *Ironbound, Major Barbara, The House, The Burial at Thebes, Big Love, Romeo and Juliet* and *The Plough and the Stars*, which also toured to the Barbican, London as part of the Abbey's centenary celebrations. Elsewhere, Aonghus has appeared in Big Telly's online *Macbeth* and *Operation Elsewhere*, and R*ight Up Your Street, Blind* (Ryots Productions); *Staging the Treaty* and *Rebel Rebel* (Anu Productions); *Traitor* (That Lot); *Run/Don't Run* by Gary Duggan; *The Judge's House, Slattery's Sago Saga* and *The Nose* (Performance Corporation); *Serious Money* (Rough Magic Seeds); *Die Fledermaus* (Opera Slam); *True Enough!* (Making Strange); W.B. Yeats' *CúChulainn Cycle* (R.H.A. Downstairs, Dublin and Riverside Studios, London); *Macbeth, Hamlet* and *Romeo and Juliet* (Second Age); *Myrmidons* (Ouroboros); *The Tempest* (Corcadorca); *One – Healing with Theatre* (Pan Pan); *An Triail* (Aisling Ghéar); *Buile an Phíce* (Amharclann de hÍde); *A Midsummer Night's Dream* and *Not a Moment to Lose* (Torn Curtain).

Film credits include the forthcoming *Báite, Róise & Frank* (Best Ensemble DIFF, Audience Award, SBIFF); *The Hurler, Whispers, The Lonely Battle of Thomas Reid* (Best Feature Documentary IFTA, Best Irish Film, DIFF 2018); *The Secret Scripture, When Harvey Met Bob, Happy Ever Afters, P.S. I Love You, The Tiger's Tail, An Cosc, Pride and Joy, Ella Enchanted, The Nephew, A Basketful of Wallpaper* and *An Díog is Faide*. Television work includes *Penny Dreadful* (Showtime); *Vikings* (History); *Murphy's Law* (BBC); *Striking Out, Prosperity, Proof* and *The Clinic* (RTÉ); *Seachtar Dearmadta, Corp & Anam, The Running Mate, Rí-Rá* and *Ros na Rún* (TG4). Aonghus also presented three seasons of the online Gaelic games show, *UB GAA TV*, and twice hosted the Irish Times Theatre Awards ceremony. A prolific voice-over artist, he has performed in numerous radio dramas for RTÉ and Newstalk, and voiced the cartoons *Duel Masters, Teen Titans* and *Legend of the Dragon* for TG4. He is also host and lead commentator for OTT Wrestling.

He is founder and artistic director of Rise Productions, whose debut show *Fight Night* by Gavin Kostick earned Aonghus the Best Actor award at Dublin Fringe Festival, where it also won the Bewley's Little Gem award. It was subsequently nominated Best New Play at the Irish Times Theatre Awards, adapted as a radio play for RTÉ, and toured extensively both nationally and internationally. Rise collaborated with Gavin again for *The Games People Play*, which won Best New Play at the Irish Times Theatre Awards. *At The Ford*, the concluding instalment in the trilogy, premiered to a sold out run at Dublin Theatre Festival.

Directing credits for Rise Productions include his critically acclaimed nationwide tour of Christian O'Reilly's *The Good Father, Weekend Warrior* by Tony Doyle, *Kicking All The Boxes* by Liz FitzGibbon, which also played the VAULT Festival, London, *Cobra's Quest,* a five-part audio drama for young people, site-specific installation *Tear Down the Walls* for Project Brand New at Dublin Theatre Festival, and the sell-out music theatre piece *Celebrating Christie*. Most recently, Aonghus directed site-specific audio drama *Bliss* for Ryots Productions, the live streamed *Clara and the Spideog* for Axis Ballymun, and was associate director on Landmark Productions' *Happy Days*. Elsewhere, he directed *Group House Wedding* for Backstage Youth Theatre; *A Picture of Us: A (sort of) Musical* for The Cup Theatre Company; *Changed* for Gumption Theatre Company, *The Greatest Show on Earth* and *Dis-played* for the Gaiety School of Acting, and both *Romeo and Juliet* and *Macbeth* as part of Text Messages. For American College Dublin he directed *Mad Forest* by Caryl Churchill; *Normal* by Caitríona Daly; and *Murder of Crows* by Lee Coffey. He created the year-long Rise Productions: Irish

Theatre Podcast project, featuring weekly interviews with leading practitioners, which quickly became the Number 1 Arts podcast on iTunes and is on the syllabus at Yale University, NUI Galway, and Ulster University. It returned in 2017 for a second series, and again topped the podcast charts. Aonghus wrote and performed the digital audio piece *Another Auld Lang Syne* for Rise, and produced and directed *Rise: Audio Drama*, two ten-part seasons of short audio plays, both of which also charted at No. 1.

In response to the Covid-19 pandemic, Aonghus launched two initiatives; Rise: Covid Commissions, a series of four brand new digital theatre works, and Rise: Platform, an online showcase for actors from the graduating class of 2020.

Rise Productions was the pilot company on Irish Theatre Institute's Accelerator Programme, a fast-track resource sharing and mentorship scheme for mid-career artists, and was Company in Residence at the Main Space in Smock Alley Theatre 2018/2019. Aonghus was a participant in ITI's Six in the Attic programme 2021/2022.

Colm Maher is the technical and FOH manager of Bewley's Café Theatre. He has designed lighting for most of the theatre's in-house productions and many touring productions. He is also venue and technical manager for Bewley's Café Theatre during the Dublin Fringe Festival.

Other lighting design work includes *Tuesday's with Morrie* at the Gaiety Theatre Dublin and the Lyric Theatre Belfast, and *Connected* at Project Upstairs. As part of the Dublin Theatre Festival he lit three of Rise Productions' plays, including *Fight Night*.

In 2021 Colm was the creator and producer of Bewley's Café Theatre inaugural Walkabout season – a series of outdoor performances set in Dublin's historic parks, as part of keeping theatre alive during the pandemic. The season was nominated for a Special Judge's Award at the Irish Times Theatre Awards.

Laura MacNaughton has worked in the professional arts sector for over twenty years in theatre, film and dance. She has worked primarily as a general manager, producer and programmer. Laura has worked at a senior level in multiple arts organisations, these include The Gate Theatre, Dublin Dance Festival and the O'Reilly Theatre. She is co-founder and creative producer of Exit Pursued by a Bear, a theatre company for young audiences. Their first work *Our Little World* (2022), was commissioned in response to the impact of Covid on primary school children. Laura is a drama facilitator and director with Belvedere College Drama Department. She currently sits on the Arts Council Peer Panel for Theatre and the Producers Working Group for the Performing Arts Forum. Laura is the producer at Fishamble: The New Play Company and previous credits include *In Two Minds* (2023); *Taigh Tỷ Teach* (2024) and *Breaking* (2024).

Jim Culleton is the artistic director of Fishamble: The New Play Company, for which he has directed productions on tour throughout Ireland, UK, Europe, Australia, New Zealand, Canada and the US, including eleven transfers Off-Broadway. His productions for Fishamble have won Olivier, The Stage, Scotsman Fringe First and Irish Times Best Director awards.

Jim has directed for companies including the Abbey, the Gaiety, 7:84, Staatstheater Mainz and the Belgrade, as well as audio plays for Audible, BBC and RTÉ. He has also directed for Vessel and APA (Australia), TNL (Canada), Solas Nua, Mosaic and Kennedy Center (Washington, DC), Odysscy (LA), Origin, Irish Arts Center, New Dramatists, Irish Rep and 59E59 (New York), as well as for Trafalgar Theatre Productions on the West End, and IAC/Symphony Space on Broadway.

Eoin Kilkenny has toured across Ireland and the world with theatre productions from Landmark Productions, Rough Magic Theatre Company, Fishamble: The New Play Company, CoisCéim Dance, Abbey Theatre and many more. He has worked at some of the best festivals at the Traverse Theatre Edinburgh during the Festival Fringe, Galway International Arts Festival, Melbourne International Arts Festival, Dublin Fringe Festival and London International Festival of Theatre. He trained as a production manager with the Rough Magic SEEDs programme, working on their productions in Dublin, Belfast and New York. He is a product of UCD Dramsoc and has completed an MA in Producing at the Royal Central School of Speech and Drama.

Archer Bradshaw is a freelance lighting technician, programmer and designer based in Dublin, working nationally and internationally. Some of his recent credits include touring relighter on Fishamble's *Outrage*; chief LX on This Is Pop Baby's *0800 Cupid* and lighting designer on Anna Newell's *Attempt to Talk with the Beginning of the World*, as part of Dublin Fringe 2024. Archer trained in The Lir Academy, graduating with a B.T. in Stage Management and Technical Theatre in 2023, since graduating he has specialised in lighting, working primarily in theatre, dance and especially in work for younger audiences, and work for those with complex needs.

Eva Scanlan is the executive director at Fishamble: The New Play Company. Current and recent producing work includes *Taigh/Tŷ/Teach*, a trilingual co-production with partners in Scotland and Wales; *In Two Minds* by Joanne Ryan, *Heaven* by Eugene O'Brien, *Outrage* by Deirdre Kinahan, *The Treaty* by Colin Murphy; *Embargo* by Deirdre Kinahan; *The Alternative* by Michael Patrick and Oisín Kearney; *On Blueberry Hill* by Sebastian Barry; Fishamble's award-winning plays by Pat Kinevane *King, Before, Silent,*

Underneath and *Forgotten* and many other productions on tour in Ireland and around the world.

Eva produces The 24 Hour Plays: Dublin at the Abbey Theatre in Ireland (2012–present), in association with the 24 Hour Play Company, New York as a fundraiser for Dublin Youth Theatre. She has worked on The 24 Hour Plays on Broadway and The 24 Hour Musicals at the Gramercy Theatre in New York. Previously, she was producer at terraNOVA Collective in New York (2012–15) and has worked on events and conferences at the New School, the Park Avenue Armory and Madison Square Garden.

Allie Whelan is the marketing, outreach and engagement manager at Fishamble: The New Play Company. Allie has worked on *Mustard, King, In Two Minds, Breaking, Outrage, Heaven* and *Fight Night* with Fishamble. She has previously worked in marketing, social media and content creation roles with Dublin Fringe Festival, Poetry Ireland, Landmark Productions, Pan Pan, Glass Mask Theatre, The RDS Visual Art Awards and Music Network Ireland.

Fight Night

For Aonghus Óg McAnally

Perhaps use sound of bell to mark the changes in days.

Monday

Skipping. Words to pattern.

No excuses. No excuses. No excuses.

Monday.

Friday nigh' is figh' nigh'.

Five more days to go.

Five more days o' sorrow.

Five more days to go.

And I'll be bet tomorrow.

No. You feckin' mump.

You're gonna win this: or at least.

You can't go in expectin' to loose.

Focus you feckin' mump . . .

Space

Da.

Da.

Dhat's what it's all about, isn't it?

Hearin' your own kid say, 'Da' for dhe fuirst time.

Pure music. Pure joy.

'Jordan' she called him.

I said 'All the neighbour's kids are called Jordan.

You can't throw a bleedin' brick

Without hittin' a kid called Jordan.'

We'll say, 'Jordan, get off that bouncy castle,

And get in for your bleedin' tea,

And we'll have a rake of the fellas.'

But 'Shelle liked it. She taught it was smart, and I wanted,

I wanted to make her happy, on account

Of tings being kind of delicate at the time.

– still are a bit –

So we have a Jordan,

And Jordan, one sunny mornin' he sez:

'Da' to me, before he ever sez, 'Ma' to her, which I reckon

She finds very aggrivatin'.

O'course, 'Shelle's been reading her bukes,

And sticks her head up triumphant, 'it's only natural!'

'Look here Dan Junior', sezs 'it's developmental.'

'You're mental' I sez, havin' the hump by way of her callin' me Junior.

But she goes on an'anyways –

Sumptin' to do with his little lips, not bein' able to get round de Mmm sound.

That's what she says, 'D' is aisier.

But I know me little boy is lookin at me and sayin', 'Da',

Like he's confirmin' sumptin' and questionin' sumptin' with dhe little wise brains he has in dhere. Like it's not just muscular – dhere's deep thinkin' in it. 'Da.' What kind of fella are you?

And I say, – not out loud or anytin'

'For you son, I'm goin' to take

The middleweight championship of the world.'

Laughs unexpectedly.

I am in me hole.

Twenty-eight. Never even turned pro.

Never boxed in the Nationals.

Not like me granda.

Not like me da.

Not like me brother.

Not like none of them.

I try to see meself in the ring with Manny Pacquiao or some such and I shudder.

No feckin' way.

So I think about it some more.

And I sez,

'For you son, I am going to represent dhe West Finglas Boxin' Club again.

At the national championships.

And I am then going to represent this country at the London 2012 Olympics.'

Like me granda and the brother. Who were all actually

Real good. (*Thought.*)

Only they were goin' for different years and cities o'course.

If Da boxed in 2012 it would be a miracle,

And if Granda boxed it would be even more so on account of him bein' dead.

But you get the bleedin' idea.

Then I think about it some more,

Who am I tryin' to impress here?

Jordan? He seems to tink pretty well of me as tings are.

I sez to myself, doan' lie to the nipper now.

Doan' say nuttin' even just between youse, dhat youse are not goin' to hold too.

Da.

Da.

My da, his da, your da

A rake a'fookin das and sons all tryin'

To impress. To prove sumptin'.

To what? Each other. That dhey're good enough for each other?

That dhey're better-an each other?

I was watchin' little Jordan,

Beltin' Tinky Winky one, the way I showed him.

The way me da showed me,

I'm lookin' past him,

To 'Shelle's little back garden on the Ratoath,

In which I am not actually official,

But I'm allowed the sleep over most nights,

As long as I leave me mates out of it and do the one night feed,

Which I only bleedin' love.

And I'm tinkin' pretty profound tings.

Dhat I can't – never could – put into words.

While 'Shelle's sayin' sumptin' about he was only to have Organix, which apparently they don't do at Lidl – thus makin me a dozy prick for goin' there, an' if he goes all ADT it'll be the faul' o' yours truly.

Mind you part of me was tinkin', must get a trampoline for the nipper – funny how the brain spins away, while it's in neutral like.

And I say to mesself:

'Feck turnin' pro.

Feck the Olympics.

Dhat's the mistake I made dhe last time – expectin' too much, tryin' to prove too much.

What I'm gonna do is try.

What I'm gonna do is get fit: dhat's all. No pressure.'

Fuck me, by the time Jordan's a teenager,

I'll be fookin' forty. Jaysus.

Jus' get fi', so the nipper won't be ashamed of his aul da.

So next mornin', I haul out me mouldy trainers, fffeeeewww-eeee.

On a greyey wet, minging sort of day, wit the clouds sittin' on the rooves.

Bringin' out the very best of the pebble dash of Cabra.

I don't bleedin' tink.

'Shelle calls from the upstairs, quiet-loud cos Jordan is still in the land of nod.

'What you up to Dan?'

Wit dhat bit of sharpness that cuts, cos it has every right to be there.

'Goan' for a run'

'Why?'

'Ge' fit.'

'That's good.' She sez, 'You should,' which is surprisingly decent of her.

So I hop the gate into the Bogey's.

Jaysus – that gym wasn't even dere de last time.

And I go to kick a couple of laps around.

And for maybe a hundred metres I feel real, real good.

A proper dad, keepin' hisself in shape, maybe tinkin' at the back of me head of pickin' up a security guard job, with a smart uniform, with a cap an' evertin.

And then I feel I bit queasy, and a bit slick-sweaty and a bit breathie.

But I feel on top of it all the same.

And then I don't feel very fuckin' good at all.

And all the burgers,

And all the fags,

And all the tinnies,

And six years of four star, fuckin' kebab in a bun with brown sauce and breakfast rolls with sweaty chips, and bottles of Bulmers and nights spent shoutin' at Man U on the TV at dhem lazy fuckin' cunts and all of that, and when was the last time I had me All Bran I don't even know, come up in a big fat lardy wave, and make tings very bleedin' bad indeed.

So I stop.

From where I am I can see across the hedge to 'Shelles window.

So I tink about the big ting.

Dhat six years ago at the age of twenty-two I was all set to box at the Nationals.

Like me bleedin' Da and his bleedin' da afore and me brother.

Got to within fifteen minutes of it ac'shlee.

And I'd thrown away me trainin' in the Bottom of the Hill, and the Heineken Bar, and when the sprit took me, at Reynard's. And dhen maybe I was tinkin' dhis girl or dhat girl looks real hot in her strapless little two-piece, and mebbie she'd fancy a tasty Finglas lad like me, and the other sor' o' trainin' can wai'.

Cos mebbbie I thought I was young and immortal and I'd always have me chance.

Or deeper I was maybe tinkin' that I didn't really want to box, and I was lookin' for any excuse to lose. Or mebbie, I did like the boxin', but I didn' like the fac' that there was no though' in me head as to why I was acshlee doin' it apart from it bein' in the way of the fambly trade. An' all sorts of head-wreckie ideas like tha'.

And then the ting happened fifteen minutes before the fight and me da looked at me cos he knew what I'd done. And I didn't fight after all.

And then for six years I really didden' do much o'nothing except scaffoldin' and burgers and lookin' for me hole.

Here's wisdom – you if ye doan' respect the girls you go with: you doan' repec' yourself. Fac'.

An-anyways, back to the Bogies, I had me hands on my waxy knees, dry heavin', and I didden' even have a mouldy bottle of water.

An' the burst o' joy o' Jordan sayin' 'Da' was wearin' off like, wha' with rememberin' all too well wha' kind o' lad I was and what kind of fighter.

When it counted, I never even made it into the ring.

And I said to meself, well, am I doin' this to impress me da at last?

An dhen I tought, well, is dhis, dhis now, ainyting to do with him n'anyways, when we haven't talked in six years?

'Go home' Dan Junior, sez the excusie voice in me head. 'Go home, have a play and watch a bit of SpongeBob' – which is surprisingly good – 'and you can always have another go tomorrow.'

And I said, stop tinkin' dhere brains, this is no time for youse. Stop tinkin' there Dan Junior, Dan Junior, Dan Junior.

This is only about gettin' a bit fit, is all. Dhat's all this is. Not for nuttin' else.

Count the steps Dan. Count the bleedin' steps.

One, two, three, four, five, six . . .

And I have to say, dhose steps, they were the hardest.

Cross fades

Tuesday

Running.

Tuesday. Fight night is Friday night.

Four more days to go

Four more days of sorrow

Four more days to go

And I'll be bet tomorrow.

Must tink of a bleedin' different end for that,

Wreckin' me own bleedin' head. That's the negative thoughts like, have to work on tha'.

Shouldn't be doing too much now – just watchin' me calories, drinkin' me water, eatin' me carbs. But you have to keep the old mind and body busy.

Turned out it was 830 steps a lap round dhe Bogies.

One lap, two lap, three lap, four.

Out the Bogies, bein' overlapped by the liddle ol' ladies with the dogs, catchin' up with dhe liddle awl ladies. Shoutin' a cheerie good mawnin' to the ladies on me way scootin' pas'. Runnin' backways chattin' wid the ladies.

The awl legs are still there, then. Happy days. Then it's out the park. –

– Ratoath Road, up over the little twisty bridge, don't get yourself run over now. Past the cheapest flats in Dublin, which used to be the most expensive so that'll teach you to buy in Flinglas.

Tolka Park, Tolka Valley, hard up Cardiffsbridge, steep enough on foot.

Past the shitty shoppin' centre, past the Leisureplex and the all the little kids with the Messi shirts and no bleedin' chance, cos they aren't even playin' for the WFTA – or maybe they have if they leave off the fags I dunno – round the Mellowes Road – hello horses. The WFTRA Hall, the WFTRA Hall, where the West Finglas Boxing Club trains.

Why I am going this way, why not down around Phibsboro, Ashington, any of those?

Because, mebbie this isn't jus' about fitness any more.

Dan Junior is coming back. Dan Junior is coming back. Might be coming back. And dhese are the streets I know.

A man needs his bit of motivation.

What am I, like, showing off me gut and me shaky legs?

Only the gut goes and the legs get muscle and I lift me
weights and I eats me Ready Brek, and Jordan learns to use
his Winnie-the-Pooh potty, and 'Shelle keeps her job in the
Superquinn when all around are losing dhere's, and she
takes up Pilates and things are good.

Exceptin' dheres no work in dhe scaffoldin', but I keep
meself busy.

Six months back, I walk into the WFTRA all on me
lonesome, and I sez to Joe,

'Joe I want to come back.'

And Joe looks at me, and sez,

'Sure Dan.'

'Sure.' He means 'Sure, I can't stop you anyhow'.

'Sure.' He means 'Sure, it's a bleedin' free country.'

'Sure.' He means 'Sure you're bleedin' coming back.'

'Fancy a bit of trainin' wha?'

'Fancy a bit of boxin' alrigh'.'

Then he sez, 'Hey Dan, say hello to Finglas's new national
champ – Kelly come over here.'

Fookin' Kelly? Me mind's a bit confused like, on account that
Kelly is a girl's name righ'? And that is righ' on account of
the fact tha' Kelly is in fac' 100% a girl.

Yep, it's bleedin' Kelly Harrington. I only used to share
Tayto sandwiches with her older sister.

'Kelly's National champ at 58 kilos.'

'Hi Dan.'

'That's great Kelly. That's really sumptin'.'

So much for me machismo.

That evenin' I come into 'Shelle's – I have me own key now – to stop her bothering to make arrangements an' all – but I'm still scrupulous that it's 'Shelle's gaffe, like.

Mind you, part of that is that if I move in official we'll lose the Allowance.

'Your dad's here,' she sez.

Dan Senior.

Who used to be Dan Junior hisself on account of his da being Dan Senior in his time.

There's supposed to be some link to Daniel O'Connell. Probably shagged me great-grannie. Apprently he was a top shagger O'Connell.

I look in the back room.

The aul' man's got his hands up and Jordan is happily whacking into them.

'Guard up! Guard up! One two, one two, that's it Jordan.'

Teachin' his grandson to box. Never axed permission.

He looks up, 'Dan, how come you never called him Dan?'

I look at him: 'Too bleedin' confusin' Dan.'

How come I don't tell him I respect 'Shelle's choice? How come I doan' tell him it's feck all to do wi' him? Why am I already in the wrong?

'Dan was good enough for you.'

Me blood is raging. What's this, happy families? I don't think so. He hasn't been round since wha'? Since ever.

'What do you want Da?'

'Out you go Jordan, play in the garden, gotta make the most of the sun.'

Jordan throws himself at him – he loves the old bastard. Kids are like dogs, they know nuttin'.

'Do you want a cup of tea Dan Senior?'

'Shelle's got that thing of behavin' like everythin' is as normal as normal, like he was always poppin' over. Like he was forever poppin' over for the awl hob-nob.

'No thanks, love, wouldn't mind a word with Dan.'

'Me and Jordan are off to the shops anyhow. Stay as long as you like.'

He may as well have said please fuck off out of your own house while I lash into me son.

Not a lot gets said while 'Shelle drags Jordan off and out they go. Pretty much nothing.

'I hear you were up at the WFTRA.'

Like a load of grannies they are up in Finglas.

'Yeh, s'righ'.'

'Keepin' fit.'

'S'righ'.'

'That's great. They've a good club going in Phibsboro.'

'Have they now?'

'Yeh, some Ukranian is in there – very good conditioning.'

'Heard there was a new club in Ashington too.'

'Lot's of good clubs around.'

'S'righ'. Only I train in WFTRA. I train with Joe Vaughn.'

'If it's fitness – the Bogies has a good gym. Maybe Gaelic.'

Yeah, cos you can hide in a team game, righ' Da?

'I'm goan' to box.' Sounds like I'm boasting, I hate meself.

'Boxing's not the sport for everyone.'

I consider belting him one. The awl man has to be what fifty-five? I'm not entirely sure I'd have him. A bit of me is still scared and I hate it.

'What age was I when you first took me to the WFTRA?'

'You were in your nappies.'

'S'righ'. The new Dan Junior. The inheritor. Only that turned out to be Sean.'

'It's not about that. Never mattered how good or bad your brother was. Look at the Nevilles.'

'Wha?'

'Well, Gary's better than Phil, but it doesn't stop Phil being a premiere league player.'

Jaysus, who'd have expected a lucid argument from the awl git.

'Sean was always an excuse for you. That's why I'm askin' you to leave the WFTRA alone, the boxin' alone. Boxin's not a sport for boys who make excuses.'

Fucker doesn't even have his hands up and me stomach is hurt.

'It happened the once. It won't happen again.'

'It happened every time.'

I measure the truth o'tha'. I roll it aroun' a bit.

'No' your business anymore is it?'

'Box out of Phibsboro if you must. Box out of Ashington. It's not like they're not good clubs.' He's nearly pleadin'.

'Tanks for dhe advice.'

He looks at me. He's evaluatin'. He's tinkin' mebbie I have changed. I guess he's been lookin' for that change for a long time. Sumptin' in his face closes. He pulls hisself up.

'Get fit Dan, that's good, maybe me and your ma will come over some day, she'd like to see the little one.'

Now I'm raging, what are they, the fuckin' royal family. In his head they are o' course.

'What was your best belt, Da?'

I bleedin' know, he bleedin' knows.

'National Champion.'

'Never tink of turnin' pro?'

Not like your da, not like your good son.

'I fought as well as I could, son. And I never missed a fight.'

Nice one Da. Now I have all the motivation I want.

'See youse on figh' nigh'.'

Wednesday

Wake up, bolt upright, and sweatin' bullets.

Look down at 'Shelle in the awl IKEA queensize and am surprised she's turned in to a horse – or a mare I suppose. Loose mane and all.

'Righ' mus be dreamin'. Realise I'm late for the National.

National Stadium that is, not the grand national, but for a moment there I give a thought of hoppin' on old 'Shelle dhere, but that'd be too weirdy.

Run down in me nicks to the secret tunnel that joins up Cabra to the South Circular.

Wonder why I've never used it before, very handy it is, in spite of the vampires what turn out to be only gaggin' for a pint of yours truly. Can't punch 'em out on account of have to keep me hands safe for the figh' – can't get me mitts cut off the fangs, like, but never-an'-mind I give the white faced bastards a few slaps and they kind of whimper away.

Then I'm in through the sign marked dressin' room and I nearly shit meself, on account of the fact that I've forgot all me gear.

The tunnel back has that kind of flat escalator ting you see in dhe old airport and it's going the wrong way, or it feels that way at least, – it's doin' that Poltergeist corridor thing anyway – so in tryin' to run back I just bollix meself and doan' get anwheres at all.

So I'm back in the dressin' room and me little demon voice sez, 'Not your faul' old son, you'll jus' have to defaul'' and the new bi' of me – the bit that changed when Jordan sez, 'Da' – sez, 'but ye came here to figh' you dozy prick.'

None of that matters though when Joe Vaughn and Da come in and start getting me set up and they have a load of spare gear on account of the fac' that me brother has died and doesn't need it anymore.

I feel terrible about that, because bizarrely I'd forgotten that he'd died and I feel more guilty about how I could forget such a ting? By the way – he's not really dead, jus' in dhe dream, which is jus' as well as I have no quarrel with Sean.

So now, it's clearly six years ago. That is it's the exact same as the last time, and I'm sittin' on the high bench yoke in me shorts with Joe bindin' me hands and Dad lookin' at me and sayin' nuttin'. More accurately, looking at me gut and sayin' nuttin'. As an aside – muscle weighs more than fat, but all the same, if you're carryin' fat, and have made the weight, then you're short or water or muscle, or in my case, both.

And it's the same old, same old as every figh' with this great pit in me stomach, only this time worse, cause I'm in no shape, an' I know I'm goan' to loose.

I'm goan' to get out in front of 5,000 punters mebbe and some bleedin' fecker is goan' to pick me off and mebbe break me nose and all cos I know and Joe knows and Da knows I haven't put in the trainin'. In point of fact I even have to hand back a Mr Whippy 99 with extra sauce so's Joe can do the hands and I'm thinkin' why doan' they just le' me go in with the ice-creeum and I'll stick that in the guy's mush, which would at least have a certain style.

And the poin' is that even if I had put in dhe trainin' I'd still loose, on accoun' of bein' not dhat good really. Me name has got me to this level, but not me, not me.

So just like last time. Just en-zackly the bleedin' same, in an out o' body way, I hops up from the couch and go straigh' over on the ankle.

'I didn' bloody mean to do it!'

'Course you didn'' sez Joe.

And Dad's head snaps into the cool calculatin' sort of expression.

It was a bloody t'ick t'ing to say. Tings are in slo-mo now so I have plenty of time to question it meself. Why di' I say I didden' bleedin' mean to do it, unless'n I actually did? Though I didn' really.

Any normal boxer would just say not much, or 'feck me ankle', or similar, but somehow I think I have to justify meself.

It's like I'm a kid arrivin' at school and a bleedin' dog *has* in fact *no joke* actually eaten his homework, but the kid instead of feelin' relieved feels guilty, on account of the fact that *tha'* was en-zackly wha' he had been hopin' for – and none of that deeply matters, cos what matters is the kid has been settin' himself up to fail either way.

Phew, hope you go' that. Won't be goin' through it again.

So my dad sez, with a voice, like God havin' a quick word with Judas on Judgemen' Day, 'Whatever excuse you like Daniel. Whatever excuse you like.'

Only, cos this is a dream, he has now transformed into Jordan and the awl look of contem' is comin' from me awl son's ancient eyes.

And I tink, hats off to the subconscious there, cos isn't that en-zackerly wha' I'm scared of?

So I tries to scramble up regardless but the shootin' pain in dhe ankle is so much I wake meself up for real this time.

'Shelle is there, her little mouth open like a bud and a little snore on her.

I wake up knowin' it's best to pull out of the figh' now so's I doan' make a fule of meself.

So's I don' bring shame on anyone else. In fac' I'm no' even thinkin', whether or not. I'm thinkin', 'Righ' how can I get out of this without looking like a prick?'

I tink to meself, hang on dhere awl son.

An' I slip downstairs and I just check back in with the basics. Feet hip width. Left foot small step forward. Forty-five degree turn. Hands up. Chin down. Knees soft. On the toes. And I just let me hands go.

Time, I tink to face facts.

Today's Wednesday.

Two nigh's from now I'm goin' into the ring. No choice at all.

So brains – stop tinkin' so much about it.

I mean what's there to be scared of really en-after all?

Thursday

Maybe put a shirt on for this one.

I push the little plastic button on Jordan's harness and haul him out of his car seat.

'Should we have bought a bottle of wine?'

'What for? Nobody drinks wine.'

'Still an' all.'

'Shelle's nervous. She has her good Marks and Sparks clothes on, make-up an' everythin'. She looks gear as a matter of fac'.

'Look it, it'll be fine. We're no' stayin'.'

She looks at me nervous. I breathe.

'Goan' up dhere an' ring the bell' I sez to Jordan.

He runs up and reaches as high as he can. Drinnngg, drinng.

'You'll be alright Dan' sez 'Shelle.

Jaysus. I can't make ou' if it's a question or an order.

I stare uppen and at the roof.

'What you lookin' at?'

'Wonderin' where the flag of truce is.'

The new painted red door opens and me ma beams down.

'And who is this little chap after comin' to visit?'

Jordan looks a bit confused.

'And what is your name?'

'Jordan' sez Jordan jus' abou'.

'Kiss yer Grannie.'

'Come in, come in.'

So that's us through the door and it's all as normal as Denny's Pie.

Only I haven't been here in six years.

Only it's Thursday and tomorrow night I'm fightin'.

Only I've no idea why I've been summoned.

As a matter of fac', I had no intention of goan' near the place, but me ma got tru to 'Shelle and 'Shelle said it would be good for Jordan to get to know his grandparents and it was all done and dusted without much input on my behalf.

In fac' my main contribution has been to say, 'We're not stayin' until I've annoyed me own head.

'Hi Dan' sez Da after doin' the decent by the rest, 'fancy a beer?' Needlin' cunt.

'Water thanks Da, weigh in tomorrow.'

'Right son.'

Is callin' me son needlin'? Dunno. Probbly calls everyone son.

But I'm off balance as it were, on account of this bein' the house me and Sean grew up in and it's all the same as then, but differen'.

Ma makes herself busy with cups of tay, and fizzy drinks and wha' no' while I try to get this whole thing straight in me head.

'Nice extension, Ma' I sez, eyein' the French doors and the new deckin'.

And then me eye glides around the photos and the trophies and the framed bits of paper an' all and slowly but surely blood kind of starts pumpin' at the back of me head cos I'm not there. Not there at all.

'Shelle and Da are messin' with Jordan as a way of gettin' over havin' nuttin' to say.

'We kept all you old trophies,' sez Ma who has a laser intuition for these tings, and she points to a glass cabinet.

'We got that in Arnotts.' Classy – should've hung on for the sales.

Sure enough, there's a number of those tinny yokes you pick up at Trophies-Are-Us, with me name punched in uneven le'ers on the base.

O' course these are entirely bleedin' dwarfed by the generations of all round success and righ' up there our Sean's Olympic bronze.

Now mebbie, you migh' think, it's only a bronze, that's what they give losers isn't it when some Cuban has sorted them out? But I'm from West Finglas. I know wha' it means to get tha'. I know what tha' means.

(*Funny/reflective.*) It means you don't have to fuckin' live here any more that's one thing it means.

'Wow,' sez 'Shelle, finally on her feet in the back room. That's a lot of trophies Mr Coyle – Coyle bein' the Dansters' family name.

'Oh we have lots of photos too,' sez Ma, 'I'll get the buke.'

'They doan' want to see that old thing.' Sez Da.

'We do,' sez 'Shelle.

'I think there's a few of Dan Junior in there,' sez Ma, with a touch of a wobble.

So Da, Ma, 'Shelle and Jordan settle in to the scrap-book of memories – all yellowed ou' of the Herald, The Indo, The Press God help us, and there's plenty of polite oohin' and aahin' and 'when was that now' goin' on.

Suddenly, Jordan goes, 'Da' and points, 'Da' he sez again to a picture, so I look over to get a look, and it's not me, it's not me at all. It's me da in his prime.

And I get a sudden bad flush, and the demon voice is sayin',
that that's what you want really isn't it son, a really daddy
who never made excuses and never ran away and even iffen'
he is a bit of a prick can show you what a real da is.

And I feel like the thing that's kept me goan' is oozing out of
me pores, cos really Jordan jus' said 'Da' once upon a time to
the first bloke he looked at and he never really knew the
man inside at all.

And in an even more retarded way I also resent that I look
anythin' like the awl man in dhe fuirst place, on account of
wantin' nuttin' to do with him no more.

Seein' me head radiatin', 'Shelle and Ma tactfully take
Jordan out into the back, to give him the grand look around
of the B&Q shed, I expec'.

'How are you feelin'?' sez Da, puttin' the buke away.

Here we go.

'Grand.'

'Who are you fightin'?'

He knows. This is jus' conversation. 'Ray Joyce from Galway.'

'He's very good. You'd want to keep away.'

I'm not sure what he means by tha', but I decide with me bad
head on me to take it the wrong way.

'Too late now.'

'He's very good on the inside, they say.'

'He's very good.'

'How's the weight.'

'Joe's been great. Bang on.'

'No excuses there.'

(*Point of no return here.*)

'Da, you've got me all wrong.'

'Have I?'

'I was never sacred of bein' hit, Da, never scared of dhat.'

'No?'

'Lead with the left you reckon Da?'

'O' course.'

'Jab and move is it?'

'Always was.'

In me mind righ', I'm three again and he has his hands up for his little fighter.

'Like that?' I flick out a jab. The awl git has his hand up and catches me fist lazily.

'Jab and move.'

'Like this?'

I flick another. He catches it, like a fly clean out of the air. He has his studdyin' luke.

'Borrow some peanuts Da?'

'Go ahead son.'

I take five dry roast in my left, throw 'em all up. Pop, pop, pop, pop – catch four clean as you like and bounce 'em off the wall. Miss the fifth.

I look around the room, with the new furniture and the semi-solid hardwood floor – I've lain enough o' them.

'Bit more room on the deckin' Da.'

'Righ' son.'

So we step out the back, with the res' of them at the other end of the garden.

'Jab an' move's the job Da?'

'It is son.'

So I break his nose for him. Beautiful, beautiful left hand lead, feet, hips, shoulders the lot. Cos I'm a lot bleedin' faster than I let on in the back room. Left the fifth nut on purpose, like. Lot faster than he ever was, I reckon. I'd love to know – could I have taken the man in the photo?

But no man can figh' his own da when both are in their prime and that's the tragedy.

So I have to make do with crackin' his awl nose – and my knuckle by the sound of it, and he's down.

I stand over him.

'I was never scared of bein' hit – I was scared of lettin' you down is all. But mebbie a man who'll go down on a jab, isn't so much worth impressin'? Wanna come back for some righ's?'

And the awl fucker, fair play to him, would o' course get up for his beating. But screams and shouts and general mayhem rules the day and the happy visit is over.

We're in the little 2000 Micra, which is all we can afford on 'Shelle's wages from the Superquinn. Even Jordan seems to know to keep it schtum, or maybe he's just missed his nap.

'Do you love me?' sez 'Shelle from nowhere.

It's a serious question. She's never axed it. I think about it.

'Yes,' sez I. 'I love you Michelle Sullivan.'

'I love you Daniel Coyle.'

I think about that a bit. It's a first.

'But I don't want Jordan to turn out like that. It's not goin' to happen.'

Hello, I sez to meself. Here comes the heave-ho. Leave your key in the jar Mr Coyle.

'I don't want to see him hit you, hate you. Why do boys have to be like that?'

'We doan'' I say, genllry trying to stand up for the male of the species.

'But you do. Look at you, look at Sean off in Manchester. Your poor mam never getting' to see her sons or her grandchildren on account of youse bastards will lamp the bleedin' heads off each other if you're left alone for a minute. That's not going to be the way it is with me and you and Jordan.'

'I won't stop him boxin' if he wants to.' Which is a stupi' ting to say but it just pops out like.

'It's no' the boxin', it's the needlin' and competin', an' havin' to be one better, and always needin' to show whose got the bigger prick an' all.'

'Jaysus, I've changed Jordan's nappies, potty trained him an' all.'

'Wha'?'

'Well I've seen his willie. It's massive – for a toddler like. No competition there.'

'Dan. What is it with you and your da?'

Suddenly it's very hard to explain. I tink nice and slow. There's sumptin' about the atmos that tells me what happens next is very, very important.

'Da put everytin' into me and Sean, righ'. And Sean had it – whatever it is – and I didden'. And I doan' know if that bit missin' was in me skills or in me mind. And it got very tangled up. Because, and righ', I'm doin' me best here 'Shelle, because I could never say, "I'm not good enough", without it soundin' like an excuse, without hurtin' me da, and so I found other excuses which hurt him even more, I tink. And mebbie it is all a bleedin' excuse, I don' know.'

'This is what I see Dan. I see a good lad, who maybe was a bit wild, but sure weren't we all, and you never went into gear or into crime or ainytin' though half of your year did and half of mine as well, and then you and me have our accident.'

'He's still awake,' sez I warnin' like.

'No we're always goin' to be honest with him. So we had our accident, and the truth is iffen we hadn't we wouldn't have been together – isn't that right Dan?'

'S'true, 'Shelle.'

'So, whatever we have now right, we've built ourselves righ'? Since Jordan came. An' I'm proud of you Dan Coyle, over the last year, I seen you get yourself in shape, and you've gone out every day looking for work, and you're doin' your feckin' FAS courses and you look after Jordan real well, and you make me tea and there's no complaints. But look-it, we're the family now, and if it all ends up with you fightin' your own son, I'm not interested and it's no good. And if it ends up that I have to pick one over the other then it's no good, and if you doan' love me most of all the people in the world then it's no good.'

'I love you Michelle Sullivan, I love you Michelle Sullivan, I love you Michelle Sullivan.'

'Dan,' she says later, lookin' up at the dark o' the bedroom.

'Yeh.'

'If you've decked your da good and proper, and you've nuttin' to prove to me or Jordan.

'Yeh.'

'What do you have to fight for?'

Friday

The Changing Room.

Friday night.

Fight Night.

Call the cops.

V/O   *Ten minutes. Next bout ten minutes.*

Twelve noon – weigh in.

Sixteen lads, all down to our shorts.

Then's it's me and Ray.

Where the fuck did he get those tats? Savage. I recognise that glow, the glow of champions – saw it enough offa Sean. Give him the look all the same, sez, 'You're mine, tanks for comin'' and I experience a surprisin' wave of joy.

No problems with the weigh in. Remember when I used to have to go off and skip and sweat off a few pints, and get down to me nicks.

This time, I'm as clean as a whistle.

Then it's a couple of raw eggs in a juice, a la Rocky, to get a bit of energy in.

Feel pretty good actually. Ray's here to claim his Olympic place, he's tinkin' about me and the nex' figh'.

I'm just thinkin' about him. Wonderin' if I can catch 'im on the tats for the laugh.

Me mind's on idle again as Joe does the rub-down. He's hummin' Spancil Hill the old fucker, but I don' need the gee-up.

I've got nerves like, bu' in an adrenily sort of way, not a shameful sort of way.

Here's the ting. A part of me always loved this, I mean, in my ideal world, I'd have been like Kendo Nagasaki – fightin' withou' revealing me true identity like. The masked boxer with no name – apart from Kendo, which I assume was made up.

What I mean is, if I hadn't of bin Dan, son of Dan, son of Dan – the next great hope for Ireland and everythin' ye now know I couldn't carry – then I'd have bleedin' loved it.

Then it's in to the old protection, for the family jewels like, and the vest, shorts and boots.

Time for the hands.

'I'll take over there Joe, I'll do the hands, like always,' sez Da, appearin' like your man in Mr Ben.

And it's not really true that he did the hands either, but I guess he has to say something to break the ice, on account of this bein' an uncomfortable moment.

He reminds me of sumptin' – then I get what – the Odlums Owl on account of the circular bruises he has around the eyes, and the bits of grey hair stickin' out of his baldy head,

V/O   *Five mintues. Next bout five minutes.*

'How you feelin' son?' he sez.

'Good Da. Sorry about the face.'

'Great jab son. You're goin' to really take it to him.

Your Ma axed me to come in.'

'Oh, righ' tell me that just in case I thought you cared on your own account.'

'I always have cared son. I always loved you. Just everything I ever said came out wrong, or you heard it wrong, I don't know.'

Full of surprises the da.

'How come you never called?'

'How come you never did?'

I'm stumped by this.

'I was waitin' on you.'

'I was waitin' on you son. To come back to us. Look, boxin' is all I ever knew, all I was ever good at. Me da taught me, and I remember when you were just a little babbie and you said me name for the first time and I said, you're gonna be a fighter and that's what I set out doin' just like my father did for me. I though I was passing on a gift, a family trade, to me lovely son like.'

'Jordan will fight if he wants to, or not if he doesn't.'

'O' course, o' course, that's a much bether way. I'm your daddy Dan, but I'm not a wise man, I'm not a smart man.'

'Da.'

'I'm no', I'm no', me brains were always in me fists. You can't expect too much from me, and you can't put too much into what I say. I'm just a bloke. So my da taught me, no excuses, that there can be no excuses in the ring, you see, and it was meant to be a lesson about life, y'know, and I'm sorry Dan, it's a style o' trainin' that mebbie should have gone out with the ark.'

'Da.'

'You remember that time when I jumped up and twisted me ankle?'

'Yeh.' He's lookin' down now.

'Well I did twist it – that was an accident.'

'I understand.'

'No ya feckin' don', That was an accident, but two years before that, I was failin', I was trainin' to fail – sorry Joe – cos'n deep inside I knew dhat iffen I tried my best, I could never still live up to the family name. The name was too much for me, So it was aisier to feck it all up and pretend to meself, I could have been good, if only I'd tried. 'Righ? Now Da, if that's done, can I axe that if you ever feel like bein' honest and open again you feck away off, cos it's bleedin' embarrassin'.'

'Sure son. It's embarrasin' for me too.'

V/O   *Next bout.*

'Here we go.'

'You've nothin' to prove to me now.'

'Jaysus Da. Don' you think I know tha'. You and 'Shelle are givin' me the hump.

Look, I'm not doin' this for you, or her, or Jordan.

I'm not doin' it for bleedin' Joe either.

I love this.

I'll tell you what I am.

I'm a Northsider.

I'm a family man.

I box out of WFTRA,

West Finglas.

I'm not a junkie.

I'm not a criminal.

I'm a boxer.

Some one has to stand up for the Northside lads,

And say we're decent people.

So now for this fecker from Galway.

Friday night.

Is Fight Night.'

Bell. Hold. Snap.

Should be an afterglow.